SONGS

- A Million Dreams Ost The Greatest Showman
- C_est La Vie - Khaled
- Alan Walker - Lily
- All I Want
- Counting Stars - One Republic
- Beautiful In White
0 - Boy With Luv BTS
1 - I See The Light OST Tangled
2 - Calum Scott - Dancing On My Own
3 - Calum Scott - You Are The Reason
4 - Charlie Puth - We Don_t Talk Anymore
5 - Christina Perri - A Thousand Years
6 - Play Date - Melanie Martinez
7 - Despacito
8 - Ed Sheeran - Perfect
9 - Ed Sheeran - Photograph
21 - Ed Sheeran - Shape Of You
22 - Counting Stars - One Republic
23 - Drag Me Down - One Direction
24 - Andy Grammer - Don't Give Up On Me
26 - Faded
27 - Game Of Thrones
28 - Twice More & More
29 - As It Was

30 - Hillsong United - Oceans
31 - Bad Guy
32 - Jennie Blackpink - Solo
34 - Believer
35 - Maroon 5 - Memories
37 - Cardigan - Taylor Swift
39 - Marshmello - Alone
40 - Matt Redman - 10,000 Reasons
41 - Blinding Lights
42 - Michael Jackson - Heal The World
43 - Michael Learns To Rock - Take Me To Your Heart
45 - My Heart Will Go On (Titanic)
46 - Ice Cream - BLACKPINK _ Selena Gomez
48 - Dynamite - BTS
49 - Pirates Of The Caribbean
50 - Richard Max - Right Here Waiting
51 - Rihanna Diamonds
52 - I_m Yours - Jason Mraz
53 - Selena Gomez - Lose You To Love Me
54 - Señorita
56 - Heat Waves
57 - Love Scenario - iKON
58 - Rockstar
59 - Say You Wont Let Go
60 - I Wanna Grow Old With You - Westlife
61 - Lucid Dreams

Hello there. Thank you for choosing us.

Enjoy the music by hitting the notes.

Surprise Everyone

Note Intervals

ALPHA

ART

A Million Dreams Ost The Greatest Showman

C'est La Vie - Khaled

Alan Walker - Lily

All I Want

Counting Stars - One Republic

Beautiful In White

Boy With Luv BTS

I See The Light OST Tangled

Calum Scott - Dancing On My Own

Calum Scott - You Are The Reason

Charlie Puth - We Don't Talk Anymore

14

Christina Perri - A Thousand Years

Play Date - Melanie Martinez

Despacito

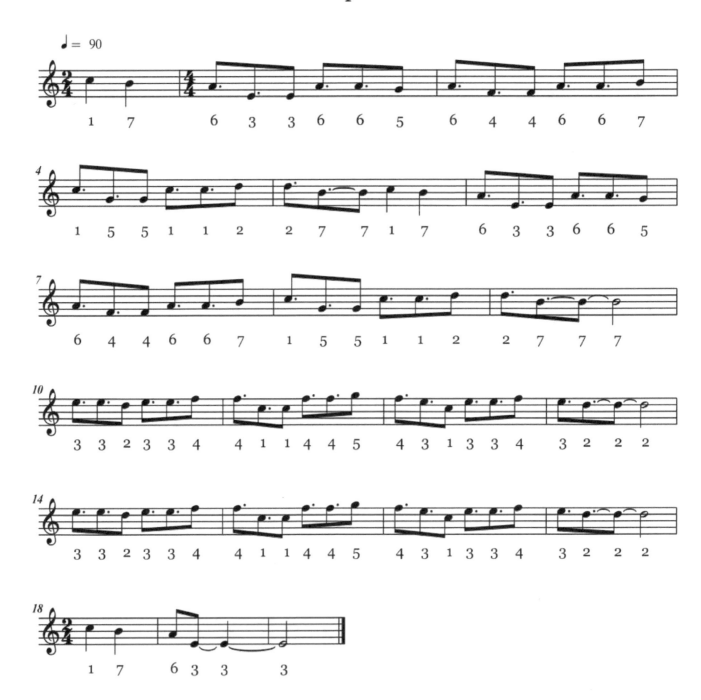

Ed Sheeran - Perfect

Ed Sheeran - Photograph

Ed Sheeran - Shape Of You

Counting Stars - One Republic

Drag Me Down - One Direction

Andy Grammer - "Don't Give Up On Me"

Faded

Game Of Thrones

TWICE "MORE & MORE"

As It Was

Harry Styles

Hillsong United - Oceans

Bad Guy

Billie Eilish

Jennie Blackpink - Solo

Believer

6 3' 2' 2' 1' 2' 2' 3' 2' 1' 6 5 6 3' 2' 2' 1' 2' 2' 3' 2' 1' 6 5 6 1' 6'

3' 3' 2' 1' 6 5 6 1' 6' 5' 6 6 6 6 6 6 6 6 6 6 6 6 6 6 6 6 6 6 6

1' 1' 1' 1' 1' 1' 1' 1' 7 7 7 7 7 7 7 7 7 7 7 7 6 6 6 6 6 6 6 6 6 6 6 6 6 6 6 6

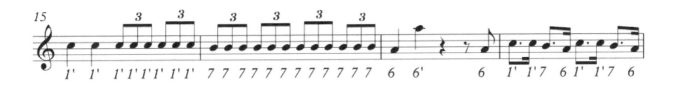

1' 1' 1' 1' 1' 1' 1' 1' 7 7 7 7 7 7 7 7 7 7 7 7 6 6' 6 1' 1' 7 6 1' 1' 7 6

6 1' 1' 7 5 6 6' 6 1' 1' 7 6 1' 1' 7 6

6 1' 1' 7 5 6 6 6'

34

Maroon 5 - Memories

Cardigan - Taylor Swift

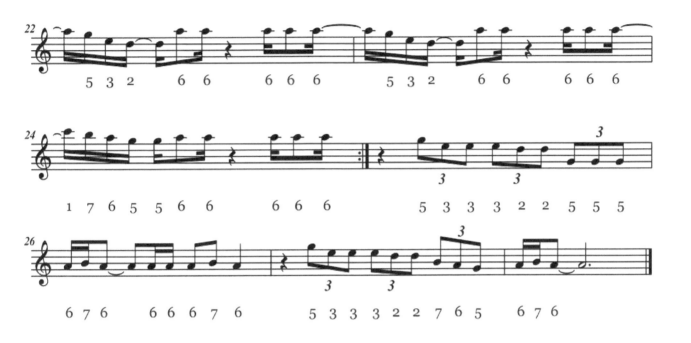

Marshmello - Alone

Matt Redman - 10,000 Reasons

3 5   6 6 5 3   2 3 2 1 6   6 1 5 3   3 1 2   2   3 5

6 6 5 3   6 7 3   1 2 3 2   2 1   1   1 5   1 1 1 6 5   7 1 1

6   1 1 1   1 2   2 2 3   3   1   4 4 4 3   2 1   2 1 2 3   2 1 6

6   1 1 1   1 2   3 2   1

Blinding Lights

Weeknd

41

Michael Jackson - Heal The World

Michael Learns To Rock - Take Me To Your Heart

My Heart Will Go On (Titanic)

ICE CREAM - BLACKPINK & Selena Gomez

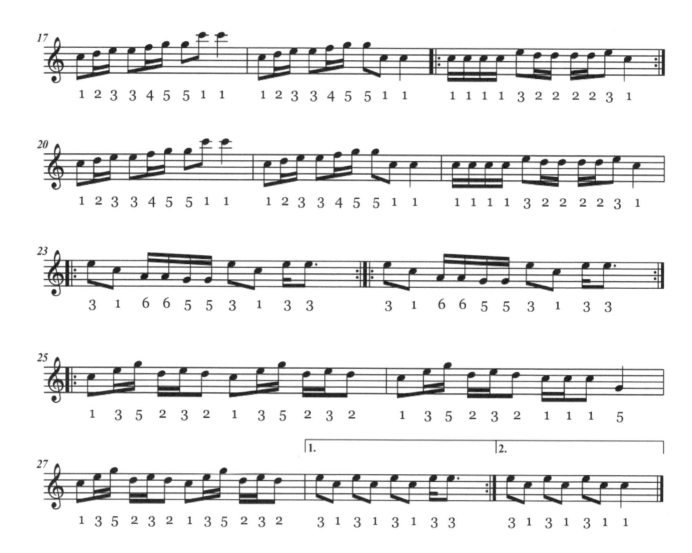

Dynamite - BTS

Pirates Of The Caribbean

Richard Max - Right Here Waiting

Rihanna Diamonds

I'm Yours - Jason Mraz

Selena Gomez - Lose You To Love Me

Señorita

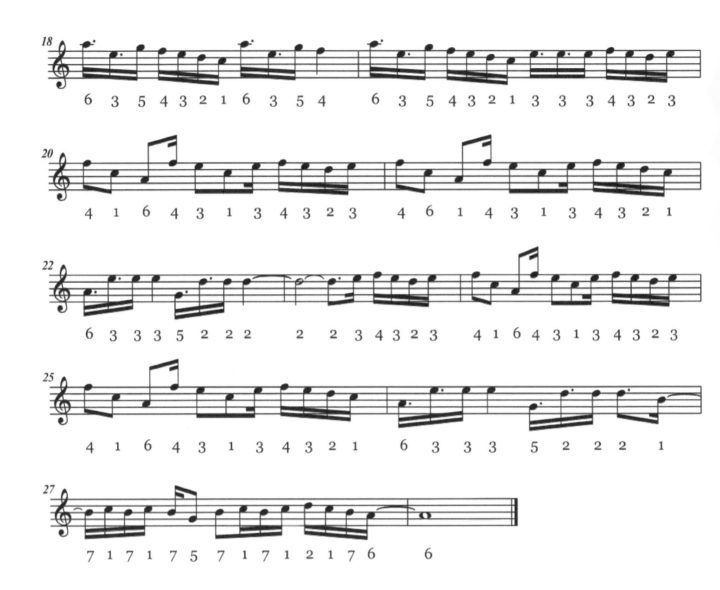

Heat Waves

Glass Animals

2' 4' 2' 4' 2'   1' 3' 1' 3' 1'   6 1' 6 1' 6   5 7 5 7 5   2' 4' 2' 4' 2'   1' 3' 1' 3' 1'

6 1' 6 1' 6 5 7   2' 2' 1' 2' 2' 2'2' 1'   2' 2' 2' 1' 2' 2' 2'3' 2' 1'   2' 2' 1' 2' 2' 2'2' 1'

2' 2' 2' 1' 2' 2'2' 3'   2' 1' 1' 1' 3'3' 2' 2'2'   2' 1' 1' 1' 3'3' 2' 2'   2' 1' 1' 3' 3' 1' 2'

2' 1' 1' 3' 3' 1' 2'   2' 1' 1' 1'3' 3'2' 2' 2'   2' 1' 1' 1' 3' 3' 2' 2'   2' 1' 1' 3' 3' 1' 2'

2' 1' 1' 3' 3' 1' 2'   2' 4' 2' 4' 2' 1' 3' 1' 3' 1'   6 1' 6 1' 6 5 7 5 7 5

2' 4' 2' 4' 2'   1' 3' 1' 3' 1'   6 1' 6 1' 6 5 7

56

Love Scenario - iKON

Rockstar

Post Malone, 21 Savage

Say You Won't Let Go

James Arthur

I Wanna Grow Old With You - Westlife

Lucid Dreams

Juice Wrld

Thank you very much for choosing me. I hope you enjoyed. waiting for your positive feedback

24455142R00038